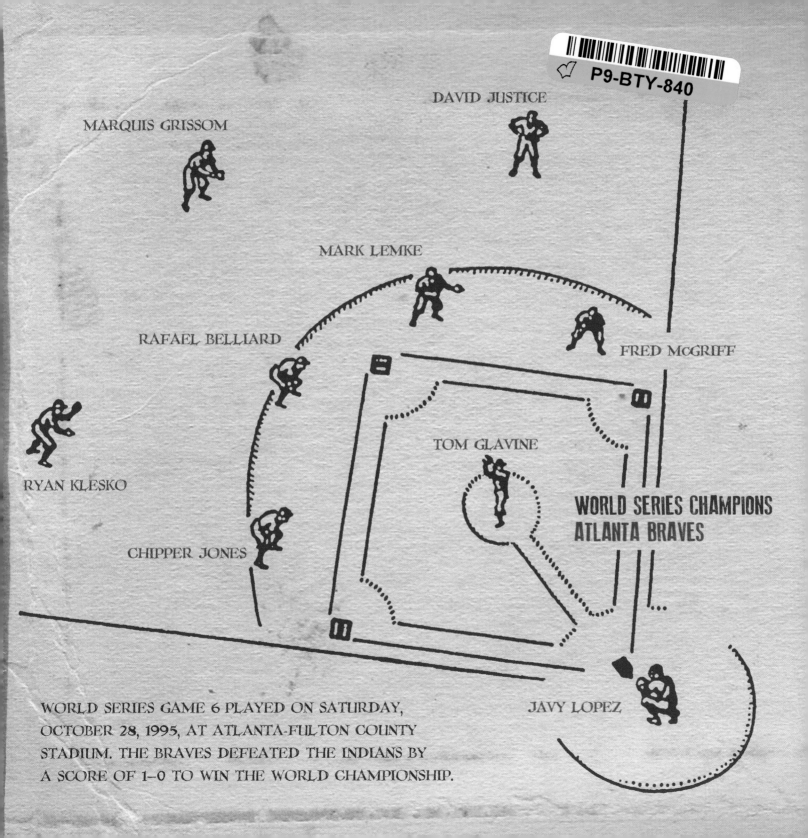

MARQUIS GRISSOM

DAVID JUSTICE

MARK LEMKE

RAFAEL BELLIARD

FRED McGRIFF

RYAN KLESKO

TOM GLAVINE

WORLD SERIES CHAMPIONS
ATLANTA BRAVES

CHIPPER JONES

JAVY LOPEZ

WORLD SERIES GAME 6 PLAYED ON SATURDAY,
OCTOBER 28, 1995, AT ATLANTA-FULTON COUNTY
STADIUM. THE BRAVES DEFEATED THE INDIANS BY
A SCORE OF 1–0 TO WIN THE WORLD CHAMPIONSHIP.

WORLD SERIES CHAMPIONS

ATLANTA BRAVES

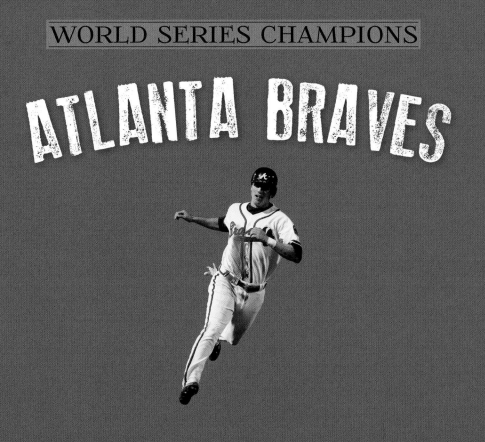

SARA GILBERT

Published by Creative Paperbacks
P.O. Box 227, Mankato, Minnesota 56002
Creative Paperbacks is an imprint of The Creative Company
www.thecreativecompany.us

Design and production by Blue Design (www.bluedes.com)
Art direction by Rita Marshall
Printed in the United States of America

Photographs by Corbis (Bettmann), Getty Images (Brian Bahr/
Allsport, Doug Benc, Matt Campbell/AFP, Kevin C. Cox, Scott
Cunningham, Monica M. Davey/AFP, FPG, Kidwiler Collection/
Diamond Images, Thomas McConville, Ronald C. Modra/Sports
Imagery, National Baseball Hall of Fame Library/MLB Photos,
Doug Pensinger, Rich Pilling/MLB Photos, John Reid III/MLB
Photos, Louis Requena/MLB Photos, Robert Riger Collection, Mark
Rucker/Transcendental Graphics, Ezra Shaw, George Silk/Time &
Life Pictures, Rick Stewart, Rafael Suanes/WireImage, Ron Vesely/
MLB Photos, Mike Zarrilli)

Library of Congress Cataloging-in-Publication Data
Gilbert, Sara.
Atlanta Braves / Sara Gilbert.
p. cm. — (World series champions)
Includes bibliographical references and index.
Summary: A simple introduction to the Atlanta Braves major
league baseball team, including its start in 1876 in Boston, its World
Series triumphs, and its stars throughout the years.
ISBN 978-1-60818-258-9 (hardcover)
ISBN 978-0-89812-809-3 (pbk)
1. Atlanta Braves (Baseball team)—History—Juvenile literature. I.
Title.
GV875.A8G48 2013
796.357'6409758231—dc23   2011051185

First edition
9 8 7 6 5 4 3 2 1

Cover: Right fielder Jason Heyward
Page 2: Pitcher Tom Glavine
Page 3: Right fielder Jeff Francoeur
Right: A Milwaukee Braves game in 1954

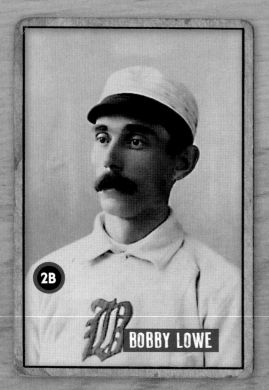

2B BOBBY LOWE

SS YUNEL ESCOBAR

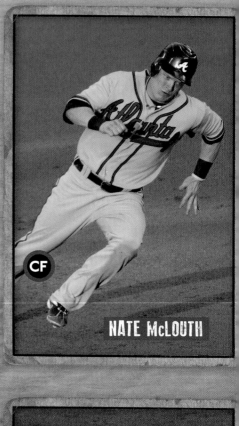

CF NATE McLOUTH

P JOHN SMOLTZ

LF LONNIE SMITH

P LEW BURDETTE

TABLE OF CONTENTS

ATLANTA AND TURNER FIELD

Atlanta is the **CAPITAL** of Georgia. It is a big southern city that is home to more than half a million people. It is also home to Turner Field, where a baseball team called the Braves plays.

ONLY POLLEN COVERS
MORE OF GEORGIA.

RIVALS AND COLORS

The Braves are a Major League Baseball team. They play against other major-league teams to win the World Series and become champions. Their biggest **RIVALS** are the New York Mets. The Braves' uniforms are red, white, and blue.

RIGHT FIELDER GARY SHEFFIELD

THIRD BASEMAN EDDIE MATHEWS

BRAVES HISTORY

The Braves started
out in Boston,
Massachusetts, in 1876.
They were called the
Red Stockings. They
became the Braves
in 1912 and won the
World Series two years
later. They moved to
Milwaukee, Wisconsin,
in 1953. In 1957, they
beat the New York
Yankees to win the
World Series again!

A BOSTON BRAVES GAME IN 1914

RF

DAVID JUSTICE

C

JOE TORRE

1B

FRED McGRIFF

OF

HUGH DUFFY

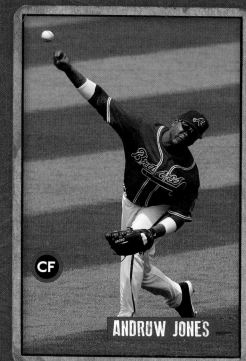

CF

ANDRUW JONES

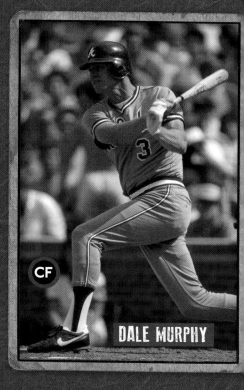

CF

DALE MURPHY

HANK AARON

In 1966, the Braves and slugging outfielder Hank Aaron moved to Atlanta. The team's new fans cheered when "Hammerin' Hank" set a **RECORD** for total home runs. They had to wait 25 years to cheer during a World Series game, though.

BRAVES HISTORY

15

GREG MADDUX

In the 1990s, the Braves and pitcher Greg Maddux went on a winning streak. They got to the World Series five times from 1991 to 1999. In 1995, they became world champions!

The Braves were one of the best teams in baseball for a long time. Manager Bobby Cox led Atlanta to the **PLAYOFFS** for 11 straight years.

BOBBY COX

WARREN SPAHN

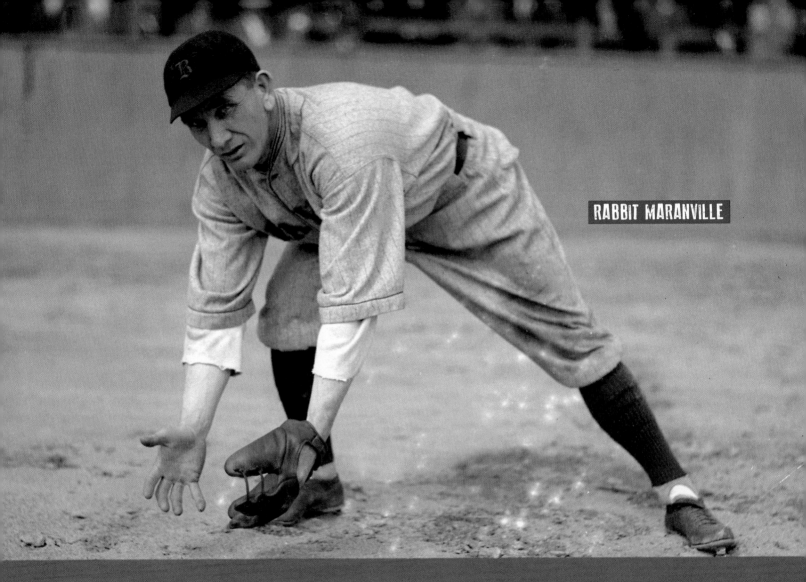

RABBIT MARANVILLE

BRAVES STARS

Speedy shortstop Walter "Rabbit" Maranville played for the Braves from 1912 to 1920. He was one of the team's first stars. Pitcher Warren Spahn threw a lot of strikes in the 1950s and '60s. He was a fan favorite for almost 20 years.

In 1964, pitcher Phil Niekro joined the Braves. His **KNUCKLEBALL** confused batters. In the 1990s, third baseman Chipper Jones became one of the best hitters in all of baseball.

Young right fielder Jason Heyward joined the Braves in 2010. He hit 18 home runs as a **ROOKIE**. The Braves hoped his powerful bat would help them get back to the World Series soon!

PHIL NIEKRO

JASON HEYWARD

HOW THE BRAVES GOT THEIR NAME

At first, people called the team the Red Stockings, the Beaneaters, and the Doves. But in 1912, a new owner named them the Braves. "Brave" is a word for an American Indian warrior. The Braves are the only major sports team in Atlanta not named for a bird.

ABOUT THE BRAVES

First season: 1876

League/division: National League, East Division

World Series championships:

1914   4 games to 0 versus Philadelphia Athletics

1957   4 games to 3 versus New York Yankees

1995   4 games to 2 versus Cleveland Indians

Braves Web site for kids:

http://mlb.mlb.com/mlb/kids/index.jsp?c_id=atl

Club MLB:

http://web.clubmlb.com/index.html

GLOSSARY

CAPITAL — the city where a state's laws are made

KNUCKLEBALL — a slow pitch that moves strangely on its way to the batter

PLAYOFFS — all the games (including the World Series) after the regular season that are played to decide who the champion will be

RECORD — something that is the best or most ever

RIVALS — teams that play extra hard against each other

ROOKIE — an athlete playing his or her first year

INDEX